Ta...
MINCE
RECIPES

Your Promise of Success

Welcome to the world of Confident Cooking, created for you in
our test kitchen, where recipes are double tested by our team
of home economists to achieve a high standard of success.

MURDOCH BOOKS

Sydney • London • Vancouver

Beef Mince

Although you can buy beef mince in several grades, fine lean beef mince will always give the best results. It is wonderful for low-fat meatballs, hamburgers and savoury meat dishes. Fresh and dried herbs, vegetables and spices of all kinds can be added to beef mince recipes – it is extremely versatile.

❖ ❖ ❖ ❖

Mozzarella-stuffed Burgers with Pesto

Preparation time:
  25 minutes
Cooking time:
  16 minutes
Serves 6

1 kg beef mince
1 small onion, finely
  chopped
1 teaspoon dried
  oregano
2 tablespoons tomato
  paste
50g mozzarella cheese
focaccia bread
2 tomatoes, sliced

Pesto
1½ cups basil leaves
⅓ cup pinenuts
½ cup grated Parmesan
  cheese
1 clove garlic, crushed
½ cup olive oil

1 Place mince, onion, oregano and tomato paste in a large mixing bowl and combine thoroughly. Divide mixture into 6 equal portions and shape into patties 1½ cm thick. Cut cheese into 3 cm squares, about 1 cm thick. With your thumb, make a cavity in the top of each of the the burgers. Place cheese in cavity and smooth mince over cheese to enclose completely. Refrigerate until required.

2 **To make Pesto:** Place basil, pinenuts, Parmesan and garlic in a food processor or blender. Blend at medium speed, adding oil in a thin stream until smooth. Transfer to a small bowl, cover with plastic wrap and store in refrigerator until required.

*Mozzarella-stuffed Burgers with Pesto (left) and
Spaghetti with Hearty Beef Ragout (page 4).*

3 Heat grill or frypan and brush lightly with oil. Cook burgers over medium-high heat for 8 minutes each side, turning once only. Serve on toasted focaccia bread with sliced tomato and Pesto.

Spaghetti with Hearty Beef Ragout

Preparation time:
  20 minutes
Cooking time:
  45 minutes
Serves 6

2 tablespoons oil
800g beef mince
1 medium onion, finely
  chopped
2 cloves garlic, crushed
1 large red capsicum,
  cut into 1 cm squares
1/3 cup tomato sauce
2 x 410 g cans
  tomatoes, chopped
1/3 cup red wine
2 medium zucchini, cut
  into 1 cm slices
1 teaspoon dried thyme
1 teaspoon dried
  rosemary
1 teaspoon dried basil
1/2 teaspoon nutmeg
750 g spaghetti

1 Heat oil in a large heavy-based pan; add mince, onion and garlic. Cook over medium heat 5 minutes until well browned and almost all the liquid has evaporated. Use a fork to break up any lumps of mince as it cooks.
2 Add all remaining ingredients except spaghetti, cover and simmer over low heat for 30 minutes.
3 Cook spaghetti in a large pan of boiling water until tender. Serve immediately with Hearty Beef Ragout and grated Parmesan cheese.

Note: Ragout is pronounced 'ragu'. It is a French word simply meaning 'stew'.

Herb Burgers with Caramelised Onions

Preparation time:
  25 minutes
Cooking time:
  46 minutes
Serves 6

1 kg beef mince
1/4 cup sour cream
1 teaspoon dried
  thyme
1 teaspoon dried basil
1 teaspoon dried
  rosemary

Caramelised Onions
1 tablespoon
  olive oil
3 medium red onions,
  sliced into rings
1 tablespoon balsamic
  vinegar
2 teaspoons honey

1 Place mince, sour cream and herbs in a large mixing bowl and combine thoroughly. Divide mixture into six equal portions and shape into 1½ cm-thick patties. Refrigerate until required.
2 To make Caramelised Onions: Heat oil in a large pan, add onions and cook over medium-low heat for 20 minutes. Onions should be very soft and golden brown. Add vinegar and honey and cook, stirring, for another 10 minutes.
3 Heat grill or frypan and brush lightly with oil. Cook burgers over medium-high heat for 8 minutes each side, turning once only. Serve with salad and warm Caramelised Onions.

HINT
Use wet hands to make shaping burgers easier. You could double the quantity and freeze half for a future meal.

Herb Burgers with Caramelised Onions

Beef and Pimiento Loaf with Cheese

Preparation time:
20 minutes
Cooking time:
1 hour
Serves 6

1 kg beef mince
2 cups (120 g) fresh
  white breadcrumbs
1/4 cup tomato paste
1 tablespoon dry
  mustard powder
2 teaspoons dried
  mixed herbs
2 garlic cloves, crushed
1 egg, lightly beaten
1 cup chopped pimiento
1/3 cup chopped fresh
  basil
2 tablespoons chopped
  black olives
250 g ricotta cheese
125 g feta cheese

1 Preheat oven to moderate 180°C. Line a 12 x 14 x 7 cm loaf tin with aluminium foil. Combine beef mince in a large mixing bowl with breadcrumbs, tomato paste, mustard, mixed herbs, garlic and egg. Divide into three portions.
2 Combine pimiento, basil and olives.
3 Press one portion of mince mixture evenly over base of prepared

tin. Top with half the pimiento mixture. Top with another portion of mince mixture, then remaining pimiento mixture, then remaining mince mixture. Bake for 1 hour or until well-browned and cooked through. Drain off liquid, stand loaf for 5 minutes, turn out, serve sliced.
4 Combine ricotta cheese and crumbled feta cheese; serve as an accompaniment to sliced loaf.

Beef and Pumpkin Risotto

Preparation time:
15 minutes
Cooking time:
15 minutes
Serves 4

60 g butter
1 tablespoon oil
1 medium onion, sliced
2 garlic cloves, crushed
350 g beef mince
2 cups Arborio rice
1 cup white wine
5 cups hot chicken stock
750 g pumpkin, cut
  into 2 cm cubes
250 g button
  mushrooms, sliced
2/3 cup grated Parmesan
  cheese
1/3 cup chopped parsley

1 Heat butter and oil in large heavy-based pan, add onion and garlic, stir-fry over medium heat for 2 minutes or until lightly browned.
2 Add beef mince, and stir-fry over high heat for 4 minutes or until well-browned and all liquid has evaporated. Use a fork to break up any lumps in the mince as it cooks.
3 Add rice, stir-fry for 1 minute. Add wine, bring to boil, reduce heat to a simmer, stir continuously for 2 minutes or until liquid is absorbed. Add a quarter of the stock and stir continuously for 2 minutes or until the liquid is absorbed.
4 Repeat process until all liquid has been added and rice is tender. Stir in the pumpkin and mushrooms after half the stock has been added.
5 Remove from heat, stir in cheese and parsley; serve immediately.

Note: Arborio rice is a large-grained white rice, available from delicatessens and some supermarkets. If it is unavailable, use long-grain rice. Cook rice just before serving.

Beef and Pimiento Loaf with Cheese (top) and Beef and Pumpkin Risotto.

Meat Pie

Preparation time:
 35 minutes
Cooking time:
 50 minutes
Serves 6

Shortcrust Pastry
3/4 cup plain flour
1/3 cup self-raising flour
90 g butter, chopped
1 1/2 tablespoons water

Filling
1 tablespoon oil
2 rashers bacon,
 chopped
1 small onion, finely
 chopped
750 g beef mince
2 tablespoons plain
 flour, extra
1 1/2 cups beef stock
1/2 cup tomato paste
2 tablespoons
 Worcestershire sauce
2 teaspoons dried
 mixed herbs
1 tablespoon dry
 mustard powder

Puff Pastry Topping
1/2 x 375 g block
 prepared puff pastry
1 egg, lightly beaten

1 Preheat oven to moderately hot 210°C. **To make Shortcrust Pastry:** Sift flours into large mixing bowl, add butter. Using fingertips, rub butter into flour for 2 minutes or until the mixture is a fine, crumbly texture. Add almost all the water, mix to a firm dough, adding more water if necessary. Turn onto lightly floured surface, knead 1 minute or until smooth. Store, covered with plastic wrap, in refrigerator for 30 minutes. Roll pastry between two sheets of plastic wrap until it is large enough to cover base and sides of a 24 cm pie plate.

2 To cook Filling: Heat oil in heavy-based pan; add bacon and onion. Stir-fry over medium heat for 5 minutes or until lightly browned. Add beef, stir-fry over high heat for 4 minutes or until well-browned and liquid has evaporated. Use a fork to break up lumps as mince cooks. Add flour, stir over heat 1 minute.
3 Add stock, tomato paste, sauce, herbs and mustard; bring to boil, reduce heat to a simmer, cook uncovered for 8 minutes or until almost all liquid has evaporated, stir occasionally, cool. Spoon into pastry shell.
4 To make Puff Pastry Topping: Roll pastry between two sheets of plastic wrap, large enough to cover pie. Brush edge of pie shell

Meat Pie

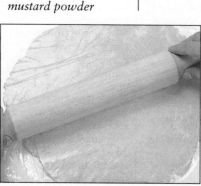

1. *Roll pastry between two sheets of plastic wrap.*

2. *For filling, add beef to bacon and onion, stir-fry until well-browned.*

with egg, place puff pastry on top, trim, press to seal. Make cuts around edge, cutting all the way through. Brush all over with egg. Use any puff pastry trimmings to make leaf shapes to place on top, if desired. Make four cuts around top of pie to allow steam to escape. Bake for 14 minutes. Reduce heat to moderate 180°C, bake a further 25 minutes or until crisp and golden brown.

3. *Add stock, tomato paste, sauce, herbs and mustard to beef mixture.*

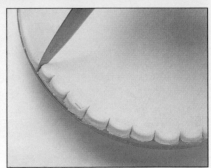

4. *Make cuts around edge of pie, cutting all the way through.*

9

Beef and Mushroom Bolognaise with Cheese Polenta

Preparation time:
30 minutes
Cooking time:
20 minutes
Serves 6

Cheese Polenta
2 cups milk
2 cups water
2 teaspoons salt
1½ cups polenta
  (cornmeal)
⅓ cup grated Cheddar
  cheese

Beef and Mushroom Bolognaise
2 tablespoons oil
2 large onions, chopped
3 garlic cloves, crushed
350 g beef mince
350 g small button
  mushrooms
440 g can tomatoes
1 cup tomato purée
1 teaspoon dried mixed
  herbs

1 Preheat oven to
moderate 180°C. Brush
an 18 cm shallow
round cake tin or pie
plate with melted butter
or oil. Combine milk,
water and salt in large
pan, bring to boil,
gradually stir in

polenta, stirring until
smooth. Reduce heat
to low, cook for
15 minutes or until
mixture is very thick,
stirring often. Add
cheese, stir until melted.
Spread into prepared
tin; bake for 20 minutes
or until firm. Cut
polenta into wedges.
2 To make Beef and
Mushroom Bolognaise:
Heat oil in medium
pan, add onion and
garlic, stir-fry over
medium heat 2 minutes
or until lightly
browned. Add beef
mince; stir-fry over high
heat for 4 minutes or
until well-browned
and liquid has
evaporated. Use a fork
to break up lumps as
mince cooks.
3 Add mushrooms,
undrained crushed
tomatoes, tomato purée
and herbs, bring to the
boil, cover, reduce heat
to a simmer; cook for
15 minutes or until
mixture has reduced
and thickened. Serve
with wedges of hot or
warm polenta.

Beef Casserole with Parsley Crust

Preparation time:
40 minutes
Cooking time:
30 minutes
Serves 4

500 g minced beef
⅔ cup fresh, white
  breadcrumbs
4 garlic cloves,
  crushed
1 tablespoon
  Worcestershire sauce
plain flour
3 tablespoons oil
3 large onions, cut into
  eighths
½ cup red wine vinegar
⅓ cup plum jam
1½ cups beef stock

Parsley Crust
1½ cups self-raising
  flour
20 g butter
2 tablespoons chopped
  fresh parsley
¾ cup milk

1 Preheat oven to
moderately hot 210°C.
Combine minced beef
in a medium mixing
bowl with the
breadcrumbs, garlic
and Worcestershire
sauce. Roll heaped
tablespoons of mixture
into balls. Place flour
on a sheet of
greaseproof paper.
Coat meatballs in flour,
shake off excess.

*Beef Casserole with Parsley Crust (top) and Beef
and Mushroom Bolognaise with Cheese Polenta.*

2 Heat oil in heavy-based pan, add meatballs in single layer, cook over medium-high heat for 4 minutes or until well browned. Turn often during cooking, drain on absorbent paper. Place meatballs into a shallow ovenproof dish.

3 Add onion to pan, stir-fry over medium heat for 2 minutes or until lightly browned. Add vinegar, jam and stock, bring to boil, reduce heat to a simmer, cook uncovered for 4 minutes or until onion is tender; pour over meatballs.

4 To make Parsley Crust: Sift flour into medium mixing bowl; add butter. Using fingertips, rub butter into flour for 2 minutes or until mixture is a fine crumbly texture. Stir in parsley. Add milk, stir with a knife until combined. Spoon rounded tablespoons of mixture evenly on top of meatballs. Bake for 30 minutes or until crust is golden brown.

Spicy Beef Empanadas

Preparation time:
30 minutes
Cooking time:
10 minutes
Makes 20

Meat Filling
1 tablespoon oil
1 large onion, chopped
2 garlic cloves, crushed
2 red chillies, chopped
375 g beef mince
1 cup tomato purée
1/2 teaspoon ground mixed spice
2 teaspoons ground cumin

5 sheets ready-rolled shortcrust pastry
1/2 cup sour cream
1 cup grated Cheddar cheese
vegetable oil for deep-frying

1 To make Meat Filling: Heat oil in heavy-based pan, add onion, garlic and chillies; stir-fry over medium heat for 2 minutes or until onion is soft. Add beef mince; stir-fry over high heat for 4 minutes or until well-browned and all liquid has

evaporated. Use a fork to break up any lumps as mince cooks. Add tomato purée, mixed spice and cumin, bring to boil, reduce heat to simmer; cook uncovered 5 minutes or until the mixture has reduced and thickened; cool.

2 Cut pastry sheets into rounds, using a 12 cm round cutter or saucer. Lay rounds out on work surface.

3 Divide Meat Filling between pastry rounds; top each with sour cream and cheese. Fold pastry to enclose filling, press edges together with fork to seal.

4 Heat oil in a heavy-based pan to moderately hot for deep-frying. Gently lower empanadas, four at a time, into oil. Cook for 2 minutes or until crisp and golden brown. Carefully remove from oil with tongs or a slotted spoon; drain on absorbent paper; keep warm in moderate oven. Repeat with remaining empanadas.

Note: Remove seeds from chillies to reduce their heat. Empanadas are delicious served with chutney or chilli sauce for dipping.

Spicy Beef Empanadas.

Potato and Almond Meatloaf

Preparation time:
15 minutes
Cooking time:
1 hour 30 minutes
Serves 8

1 kg beef mince
1 cup (60 g) fresh white breadcrumbs
2 sticks celery, finely chopped
1 large onion, finely chopped
1 tablespoon grated fresh ginger
2 garlic cloves, crushed
1 tablespoon curry powder
1 tablespoon garam masala
2/3 cup plain yoghurt
2 eggs, lightly beaten
2 cups mashed potato
2/3 cup flaked almonds

1 Preheat oven to moderate 180°C. Brush 20 cm round cake tin with melted butter or oil. Combine beef mince in large bowl with breadcrumbs, celery, onion, ginger, garlic, curry powder, garam masala, yoghurt and egg. Press into tin, bake 1 hour 15 minutes or until well-browned. Pour off liquid; turn loaf onto oven tray.
2 Spread loaf all over with potato; press almonds over potato.

Increase oven temperature to moderately hot 210°C ; bake loaf 15 minutes or until almonds are golden brown. Cut into wedges to serve.

Beef and Vermicelli Stir-fry

Preparation time:
30 minutes
Cooking time:
15 minutes
Serves 4

Meatballs
500 g beef mince
4 spring onions, chopped
1 tablespoon soy sauce
2 cups (120 g) fresh white breadcrumbs
1 egg, lightly beaten
oil for shallow frying

100 g dried vermicelli
1 tablespoon oil
1 tablespoon sesame oil
1 large onion, cut into eighths
1 large red capsicum, seeded, cut into strips
2 cups sliced cabbage
2 garlic cloves, crushed
2 teaspoons grated ginger
230 g can sliced bamboo shoots, drained
3 teaspoons cornflour
1 1/2 cups chicken stock
1 tablespoon soy sauce
1/4 cup plum sauce

1 **To make Meatballs:** Combine beef mince in mixing bowl with spring onion, soy sauce, breadcrumbs and egg. Roll tablespoons of mixture into balls. Heat oil in heavy-based pan. Add meatballs in single layer, cook on all sides over medium heat 4 minutes or until cooked through and well-browned; drain on absorbent paper.
2 Place vermicelli in a bowl, cover with hot water, stand 10 minutes, drain, set aside.
3 Heat oil and sesame oil in heavy-based pan, add onion and capsicum, stir-fry over high heat 2 minutes. Add cabbage, garlic and ginger, stir-fry 1 minute. Add bamboo shoots and meatballs, stir-fry for 2 minutes.
4 Add cornflour, blended with a little stock, remaining stock, soy sauce and plum sauce, stir-fry until vegetables are tender and meatballs heated through. Add vermicelli, stir until combined.

Potato and Almond Meatloaf (top) and Beef and Vermicelli Stir-fry

Carpetbag Burgers with Horseradish Cream

Preparation time:
20 minutes
Cooking time:
16 minutes
Serves 6

750 g beef mince
1 cup (60 g) fresh white
   breadcrumbs
½ teaspoon finely grated
   lemon rind
5 drops Tabasco
   sauce
1 egg, lightly beaten
6 oysters

Horseradish Cream
½ cup sour cream
2 teaspoons horseradish
   relish

1 Place mince, breadcrumbs, lemon rind, Tabasco and egg in a large mixing bowl and combine thoroughly. Divide mixture into six equal portions and shape into patties 1½ cm thick. With your thumb, make a cavity in the top of each burger. Place an oyster in the cavity and smooth mince over oyster to enclose completely. Refrigerate until required.
2 **To make Horseradish Cream:** Combine ingredients in a small bowl and refrigerate until required.

3 Heat grill or frypan, brush lightly with oil. Cook burgers over medium-high heat for 8 minutes each side, turning once only. Serve on hamburger bun with shredded lettuce and Horseradish Cream.

Brandied Beef and Mushroom Puffs

Preparation time:
30 minutes
Cooking time:
30 minutes
Serves 4

500 g beef mince
1 medium onion, finely
   chopped
¼ cup tomato paste
2 tablespoons chopped
   fresh rosemary
1 tablespoon oil
30 g butter
375 g block puff pastry
milk for glazing

Filling
60 g butter
1 stick celery, finely
   chopped
125 g mushrooms,
   finely chopped
2 garlic cloves, crushed
⅓ cup brandy
½ cup thickened cream

1 Preheat oven to moderately hot 210°C. Brush oven tray with

melted butter or oil. Combine beef mince, onion, tomato paste and rosemary in bowl. Divide mixture into four; roll each portion into log shape about 12 cm long.
2 Heat oil and butter in heavy-based pan; add logs. Cook over medium heat 4 minutes to seal, turn occasionally. Reduce heat to low, cook 5 minutes or until cooked through; turn occasionally. Remove from pan; drain on absorbent paper; cool.
3 **To make Filling:** Heat butter in small pan, add celery, mushrooms and garlic, stir-fry over medium heat 2 minutes or until vegetables are tender. Add brandy and cream, stir over heat for 2 minutes or until mixture has reduced and thickened; cool.
4 Divide pastry into four; roll each portion out on a lightly floured surface to make a 25 x 15 cm rectangle. Cut out corners. Spread Filling along centre, place logs on top of Filling. Brush pastry with milk. Wrap pastry around logs, press to seal. Place seam-side down on prepared tray, brush with milk. Bake for 30 minutes or until golden brown.

Carpetbag Burgers with Horseradish Cream (top) and Brandied Beef and Mushroom Puffs.

Stuffed Tomatoes

Preparation time:
  20 minutes
Cooking time:
  40 minutes
Serves 6

¼ cup burghul (cracked wheat)
⅓ cup hot water
1 tablespoon oil
1 small onion, finely chopped
500 g beef mince
50 g sundried tomatoes, finely sliced
2 tablespoons tomato paste
1 tablespoon barbecue sauce
1 teaspoon dried oregano
1 tablespoon finely chopped parsley
6 large firm tomatoes
2 teaspoons olive oil

1 Preheat oven to 180°C. Brush a deep baking dish with oil. Place burghul in a small bowl and add hot water. Set aside for 15 minutes. Squeeze excess moisture from burghul. Heat oil in a heavy-based frypan; add onion and mince, cook for 5 minutes. Use a fork to break up any lumps as mince cooks. Remove from heat and drain excess liquid. Transfer to mixing bowl.

2 Add burghul, sundried tomatoes, tomato paste, barbecue sauce and herbs to mince mixture and combine thoroughly.

3 Cut a 2 cm slice from the base of each tomato, and scoop out seeds and membrane. Fill cavity with mince mixture, replace tops.

4 Brush each tomato all over with oil, and place in prepared dish about 3 cm apart. Bake for 35 minutes.

Stuffed Tomatoes.

1. Heat oil in heavy-based frypan, add onion and mince.

2. Add burghul, sundried tomatoes, tomato paste, barbecue sauce and herbs.

3. *Scoop seeds and membrane from base of tomatoes.*

4. *Brush each tomato all over with oil, place in baking dish.*

Meatball Paprika with Noodles

Preparation time:
25 minutes
Cooking time:
50 minutes
Serves 6

850 g beef mince
1/2 cup (30 g) fresh
  white breadcrumbs
1 egg, lightly beaten
1/2 teaspoon ground
  black pepper
1 tablespoon dried
  oregano
2 tablespoons oil
2 tablespoons oil,
  extra
1 large onion, sliced
2 medium green
  capsicums, cut into
  1 cm strips
1 tablespoon plain
  flour
2 teaspoons paprika
1 teaspoon caraway
  seeds
2 cups beef stock
415 mL can tomato
  purée
2 bay leaves
2 tablespoons tomato
  paste
1/4 cup sour cream
750 g fettucine

1 Place mince, breadcrumbs, egg, pepper and oregano into a large mixing bowl and combine thoroughly. Roll heaped tablespoonfuls of mixture into 30 balls.

2 Heat oil in a large non-stick frypan. Cook meatballs over medium-high heat for 5 minutes, shaking pan occasionally, until brown all over. Cook in batches; do not overcrowd pan. Remove from pan.
3 Heat extra oil in a large pan. Add onion and capsicum and stir-fry for 2 minutes or until just soft. Reheat juices from meatballs in frypan; add flour, paprika and caraway seeds, stir-fry for 2 minutes. Add stock gradually to frypan, stirring over low heat for 2 minutes. Combine stock mixture, tomato purée and bay leaves with vegetables in large pan. Bring to the boil, add the meatballs, cover and simmer over low heat for 20 minutes. Add tomato paste, and simmer uncovered a further 15 minutes; stir occasionally.
4 Cook fettucine in a large pan of boiling water until tender. Drain. Pour sour cream over meatballs; gently mix through and serve immediately with the fettucine.

Beef Patties with Tomato Spice Butter

Preparation time:
30 minutes
Cooking time:
20 minutes
Serves 4

500 g beef mince
1 cup cooked rice
2 teaspoons curry
  powder
2 tablespoons oil

Tomato Spice Butter
1 tablespoon oil, extra
1 large onion, chopped
2 garlic cloves,
  crushed
1 tablespoon grated
  ginger
2 teaspoons ground
  cumin
2 teaspoons ground
  coriander
2 teaspoons French
  mustard
2 teaspoons sugar
1 tablespoon tomato
  paste
440 g can tomatoes
1/2 cup water
60 g butter

1 Combine beef mince in a large mixing bowl with rice and curry powder. Roll mixture into eight equal patties.
2 Heat oil in large heavy-based pan. Add patties in single layer; cook over medium heat

Meatball Paprika with Noodles (top) and Beef Patties with Tomato Spice Butter.

for 3 minutes on each side or until cooked through. Remove from pan, drain on absorbent paper; keep warm.

3 To make Tomato Spice Butter: Heat extra oil in medium pan, add onion, garlic and ginger, stir-fry for 2 minutes or until onion is soft. Add cumin, coriander, mustard, sugar, tomato paste, undrained tomatoes and water, bring to boil, cover, reduce heat to a simmer, cook for 10 minutes or until sauce has reduced and thickened. Remove from heat, pour into blender or food processor bowl, blend until smooth. Add butter, blend until combined; pour over patties to serve.

21

Pork and Veal Mince

Y ou can buy pork mince and veal mince separately and mix them together in proportions to suit yourself, or buy the combined mixture from your butcher. Pork and veal mince is especially good as a filling for ravioli and cannelloni, and can be used for excellent light sauces for pasta. Fresh herbs, particularly sage and basil, are delicious with pork and veal mince. And, of course, you can use either meat separately.

❖ ❖ ❖ ❖

Italian-style Stuffed Zucchini

Preparation time:
  15 minutes
Cooking time:
  30 minutes
Serves 4

4 large zucchini
2 tablespoons oil
1 large onion, chopped
2 rashers bacon
2 garlic cloves, crushed
250 g pork and veal mince
1½ cups cooked rice
1 cup tomato purée
1 teaspoon dried mixed herbs
½ teaspoon chilli powder
2 tablespoons grated fresh Parmesan cheese

1 Preheat oven to moderate 180°C. Brush an oven tray with melted butter or oil. Cut the zucchini in half lengthways. Using a small spoon, carefully scoop out flesh; chop the flesh roughly.
2 Heat oil in a heavy-based pan, add onion, chopped bacon and garlic, stir-fry over medium heat for 3 minutes or until lightly browned. Add the combined pork and veal mince and stir-fry over high heat for 4 minutes or until it is well-browned and all the liquid has evaporated. Use a fork to break up any lumps as mince cooks.

Italian-style Stuffed Zucchini (top) and Spicy Spanish Sausages with Bean Salad (page 24).

3 Add rice, tomato purée, herbs, chilli and reserved chopped zucchini, stir-fry over medium heat 1 minute. Spoon into zucchini shells, sprinkle with cheese. Place on prepared tray, bake for 30 minutes or until zucchini are tender.

Spicy Spanish Sausages with Bean Salad

Preparation time:
  20 minutes
Cooking time:
  10 minutes
Serves 6

1 kg pork mince
2 cloves garlic, crushed
1 teaspoon chilli powder
1 teaspoon ground cumin
1 teaspoon onion salt
1 tablespoon
  Worcestershire sauce

Bean Salad
2 x 430 g cans
  three-bean mix
1 medium red onion,
  finely sliced
1/3 cup olive oil
2 tablespoons cider
  vinegar
1 teaspoon honey
1/2 teaspoon Dijon
  mustard

1 Place mince, garlic, spices and sauce into a large mixing bowl and combine thoroughly.

Divide into 12 portions and shape into sausages about 12 cm long.
2 **To make Salad:** Rinse and drain beans. Combine in a medium mixing bowl with onion. Place oil, vinegar, honey and mustard in a small jar. Shake vigorously for 1 minute or until combined. Pour over bean mixture.
3 Heat grill or frypan and brush lightly with oil. Cook sausages over medium-high heat for 10-12 minutes, turning occasionally. Serve with Bean Salad.

Pork Frittata with Spicy Apples

Preparation time:
  25 minutes
Cooking time:
  40 minutes
Makes 12

1 large potato (350g),
  cut into chunks
500 g pork mince
1 medium onion, finely
  chopped
2 teaspoons dried sage
2 tablespoons fresh
  chives, finely chopped
1 egg, lightly beaten
pepper to taste
2 teaspoons oil

Spiced Apples
3 medium green apples
20 g butter
1/2 cup water
1/2 teaspoon ground
  ginger
1/2 teaspoon mixed spice
2 tablespoons fruit
  chutney

1 Cook potato in boiling water until just tender. Mash until chunks are just broken up; do not overmash. Place potato, mince, onion, herbs and egg into bowl and combine thoroughly. Form into a flat disc 20 cm across.
2 Brush 20 cm non-stick frypan lightly with oil. Cook Frittata over medium heat for 8 minutes. To turn Frittata, slide from pan onto a dinner plate. Wipe pan with paper towel, brush lightly with oil and place upside down over plate. Invert plate over frypan to replace Frittata. Cook this side another 8 minutes. Serve with Spiced Apples.
3 **To make spiced Apples:** Peel, core and slice apples thinly. Heat butter in small pan and stir-fry apples over low heat for 2 minutes. Add water, spices and chutney; cover, simmer for 15 minutes, stirring occasionally.

Pork Frittata with Spicy Apple

Pork and Veal Potato Bake

Preparation time:
  15 minutes
Cooking time:
  30 minutes
Serves 4

1 tablespoon oil
30 g butter
2 leeks, sliced
400 g pork and veal
  mince
125 g pepperoni,
  chopped
1 tablespoon chopped
  fresh oregano
4 medium new potatoes
  (about 1 kg)
½ cup grated Cheddar
  cheese
1¼ cups cream

1 Preheat oven to moderate 180°C. Heat oil and butter in pan, add leeks, stir-fry over medium heat for 2 minutes. Add pork and veal mince and pepperoni, stir-fry over high heat for 4 minutes or until well-browned and all the liquid has evaporated. Use a fork to break up any lumps as mince cooks, stir in oregano, set aside.
2 Peel potatoes, cut into 3 mm slices. Cook in a large pan of rapidly boiling water for 3 minutes or until just tender, drain, rinse under cold water, drain again.

3 Lay half potato slices over base of a 1.5 litre heatproof dish, top with mince mixture. Lay remaining potato slices over top, sprinkle with cheese, pour over cream. Bake for 30 minutes.

Spicy Grilled Meatballs

Preparation time:
  20 minutes
Cooking time:
  15 minutes
Serves 4

750 g pork and veal
  mince
1 cup (about 60 g) fresh
  white breadcrumbs
2 garlic cloves, crushed
8 spring onions, finely
  chopped

Marinade
½ cup plain yoghurt
1 small onion,
  chopped
2 red chillies, chopped
1 teaspoon grated fresh
  ginger
1 teaspoon ground
  turmeric
3 teaspoons ground
  paprika
1 teaspoon ground
  garam masala
1 teaspoon finely grated
  lemon rind
1 tablespoon lemon
  juice

1 Combine pork and veal mince in medium mixing bowl with breadcrumbs, garlic and spring onions. Roll heaped tablespoons of mixture into eight balls, place in a shallow baking dish.
2 **To make Marinade:** Place yoghurt in food processor bowl or blender with onion, chilli, ginger, turmeric, paprika, garam masala, lemon rind and juice. Blend for 1 minute or until smooth.
3 Pour marinade over meatballs, store covered with plastic wrap in refrigerator for several hours or overnight, turning occasionally. Drain meatballs and reserve the marinade.
3 Place the meatballs on a cold, lightly oiled grill tray. Cook under high heat for 15 minutes or until meatballs are cooked through and well browned. Turn meatballs occasionally and brush with the reserved marinade several times during cooking.

Note: The meatballs can be marinated a day ahead and cooked just before serving.
Unsuitable to freeze.

---

*Pork and Veal Potato Bake (top) and
Spicy Grilled Meatballs.*

Pork and Veal Ravioli with Creamy Sauce

Preparation time:
1 hour
Cooking time:
5 minutes
Serves 4

Dough
2 cups plain white flour
2 eggs, lightly beaten
2 tablespoons oil
1/3 cup water

Filling
1 tablespoon oil
4 spring onions
3 garlic cloves
250 g pork and veal mince
1 egg, lightly beaten

Sauce
60 g butter
1 cup mascarpone cheese
2 tablespoons fresh sage
1/3 cup grated Parmesan
1/3 cup almond slivers

1 To make Dough: Place flour, eggs, oil and water in a food processor bowl. Process for 5 seconds or until mixture comes together in a ball. Leave covered in plastic wrap in refrigerator 15 minutes. If food processor is unavailable, combine ingredients in large mixing bowl, using your fingertips.

2 To make Filling: Heat oil in heavy-based pan, add finely chopped spring onions and crushed garlic, stir-fry over medium heat for 2 minutes. Add mince, stir-fry over high heat for 4 minutes or until well browned and all liquid has evaporated. Use a fork to break up any lumps as mince cooks; cool, stir in egg.

3 Roll half the dough out very thinly (about 1mm) onto a lightly-floured surface. Use a large sharp knife to cut dough into 6 cm squares. Brush half the squares very lightly with water, place a teaspoonful of filling onto each. Top each with another square, (on the diagonal), press down firmly to seal filling inside. Place in a single layer onto well-floured oven trays. Repeat with remaining Dough and Filling.

4 To make Sauce: Melt butter in medium pan, add mascarpone cheese, stir over medium heat until melted. Add Parmesan and chopped sage and heat, stirring, for 1 minute.

Cook ravioli in a large pan of rapidly boiling water for 5 minutes or until tender. Drain, serve with Sauce, sprinkle with toasted almond slivers.

Pork and Veal Ravioli with Creamy Sauce.

1. Process dough until the mixture comes together in a ball.

2. For Filling, stir-fry mince with spring onions and garlic.

3. Place a teaspoon of the Filling onto each dough square.

4. For Sauce, melt butter and mascarpone, stir in Parmesan and sage.

Creamy Pork and Veal Meatballs

Preparation time:
 15 minutes
Cooking time:
 20 minutes
Serves 4

500 g pork and veal
 mince
1/4 cup chopped chives
2 garlic cloves, crushed
1 cup (about 60 g) fresh
 breadcrumbs
1 egg, lightly beaten
2 tablespoons oil
2 large red onions, cut
 into eighths
1 cup chicken stock
1 cup white wine
1 cup sour cream
1/4 cup chopped parsley

1 Combine pork and
veal mince in mixing
bowl with chives, garlic,
breadcrumbs and egg.
Roll tablespoons of
mixture into balls.
2 Heat oil in
heavy-based pan, add
meatballs in a single
layer. Cook over medium
heat for 4 minutes or
until browned, turning
occasionally, drain on
absorbent paper.
3 Add onion to pan;
stir-fry over medium heat
until lightly browned.
Add stock and wine,
bring to boil, reduce heat

to low; cook uncovered
10 minutes or until
mixture has reduced
by half.
4 Add sour cream and
meatballs, cook further
10 minutes or until sauce
is thick and meatballs
cooked through; gently
stir in parsley.

Continental Pork and Veal Roll

Preparation time:
 20 minutes
Cooking time:
 45 minutes
Serves 4

500 g pork and veal
 mince
1/2 cup (about 30 g) fresh
 breadcrumbs
1 egg, lightly beaten
1 tablespoon chopped
 parsley
12 English spinach
 leaves, stalks removed
125 g sliced salami
4 slices prosciutto
1 cup (about 60 g) fresh
 breadcrumbs, extra
4 spring onions,
 chopped
2 tablespoons grated
 fresh Parmesan cheese
2 teaspoons grated
 lemon rind
2 tablespoons lemon juice
1 cup sour cream
2 tablespoons French
 mustard

1 Preheat oven to
moderately hot 210°C.
Brush an oven tray with
melted butter or oil.
Combine pork and
veal mince in a large
mixing bowl with
breadcrumbs, half the
beaten egg and all the
parsley. Place a large
sheet of aluminium foil
on work surface. Press
mince mixture over foil
to a 20 x 25 cm
rectangle.
2 Lay spinach over
mince and top with
salami and prosciutto.
3 Combine extra
breadcrumbs in a small
mixing bowl with
remaining beaten egg,
spring onion, cheese,
lemon rind and juice,
press evenly over
prosciutto. Using foil as
a lever, carefully roll up
from the long side. Place
seam-side-down on
prepared tray, press ends
together to seal, cover
with foil. Bake for
40 minutes, remove foil,
drain off liquid, bake
further 5 minutes or
until browned.
4 Combine sour cream
and mustard, serve with
sliced Pork and Veal Roll.

Note: The roll can be
prepared up to 8 hours
ahead and cooked just
before serving. It is also
delicious served cold.
After cooking, the roll
can be frozen for up
to 2 months.

*Creamy Pork and Veal Meatballs (top) and
Continental Pork and Veal Roll.*

Pizza Loaf

Preparation time:
 30 minutes
Cooking time:
 1 hour 15 minutes
Serves 6

1 unsliced white tank
 loaf (cylindrical) of
 bread
250 g pork and veal
 mince
125 g salami, finely
 chopped
2 spring onions, chopped
1 small green capsicum,
 chopped
440 g can pineapple
 pieces, drained
2 tablespoons chopped
 black olives
¼ cup tomato paste
1 tablespoon fresh thyme
 leaves
4 slices Cheddar cheese

1 Preheat oven to
moderate 180°C. Cut
one end off loaf of bread,
reserve. Scoop out
centre, leaving a 1 cm
layer; use the centre to
make breadcrumbs.
You will need 1 cup
fresh breadcrumbs for
this recipe.
2 Combine the
breadcrumbs in large
mixing bowl with pork
and veal mince, salami,
spring onions, capsicum,
pineapple, olives, tomato
paste and thyme. Spoon
into loaf, replace end of
loaf, hold in position
with toothpicks.
3 Place loaf on an oven
tray, cover with
aluminium foil, bake for
40 minutes. Remove foil,
bake for a further
30 minutes. Lay cheese
slices over top, bake for
5 minutes or until cheese
has melted, stand
5 minutes, serve sliced.

Pork and Veal Kiev

Preparation time:
 30 minutes
Cooking time:
 25 minutes
Serves 4

125 g camembert
 cheese
2 garlic cloves,
 crushed
1 tablespoon French
 mustard
2 tablespoons chopped
 fresh parsley
500 g pork and veal
 mince
1 cup (about 60 g) fresh
 white breadcrumbs
1 egg, lightly beaten
2 tablespoons oil
8 sheets filo pastry
90 g butter, melted
⅓ cup flaked almonds

1 Preheat oven to
moderate 180°C. Brush
an oven tray with melted
butter or oil. Place cheese
in a small bowl, mash
with a fork. Add garlic,
mustard and parsley,
combine well.
2 Combine pork and
veal mince in a medium
bowl with breadcrumbs
and egg. Press quarter of
the mince mixture into a
rectangle approximately
10 x 8 cm. Spoon
quarter of the cheese
mixture along the centre,
enclose completely with
mince mixture, cover
with plastic wrap,
refrigerate for about 30
minutes. Repeat with
remaining three portions
of meat and cheese.
3 Heat oil in
heavy-based pan, add
pork and veal rolls, cook
over medium heat for
4 minutes or until
well-browned on all
sides, drain on absorbent
paper, cool.
4 Place a sheet of filo
pastry onto work
surface, brush all over
with melted butter, top
with another sheet of filo
pastry, brush with butter.
Fold pastry crossways in
half. Place a pork and
veal roll on one end of
pastry, roll up, tucking
in ends. Repeat with
remaining pastry and
pork and veal rolls to
give four parcels.
5 Place parcels onto
prepared tray, brush
with butter, sprinkle tops
with almonds. Bake for
25 minutes or until
golden brown.

Pizza Loaf (top) and Pork and Veal Kiev.

Lamb Mince

Many Middle-eastern dishes are made from minced lamb – koftas, meatballs, filo pastries, and little vine-wrapped parcels. Fresh mint, dried cumin and pinenuts are the most commonly used flavourings. But minced lamb can also be delicious used in hamburgers, pies and pasta sauces and casseroles.

❖ ❖ ❖ ❖

Middle Eastern Lamb Pita Pockets

Preparation time:
  20 minutes
Cooking time:
  10 minutes
Serves 6

2 tablespoons oil
1 large onion, chopped
500 g lamb mince
*1 medium (250 g)
  eggplant, cut into
  1 cm cubes*
*2 teaspoons garam
  masala*
1/2 cup chicken stock
1/2 cup tomato purée
1/3 cup sultanas
2 tablespoons pinenuts
6 small pita pockets
1 large carrot, grated
6 slices beetroot
*2 cup finely sliced
  lettuce*
1/2 cup plain yoghurt

1 Heat oil in heavy-based pan, add onion, stir-fry over medium heat for 2 minutes or until onion is lightly browned. Add lamb mince, stir-fry over high heat for 4 minutes or until well-browned and all liquid has evaporated. Use a fork to break up any lumps as mince cooks.
2 Add eggplant, garam masala, stock, tomato purée and sultanas, bring to boil, reduce heat to a simmer, cover; cook for 10 minutes or until eggplant is tender and mixture has reduced and thickened. Stir in pinenuts.
3 Cut pita pockets in half, spoon in lamb filling, top with beetroot, carrot, lettuce and yoghurt.

Middle Eastern Lamb Pita Pockets (top) and Lamb and Yoghurt Diamonds with Tabbouleh (page 36).

Lamb and Yoghurt Diamonds with Tabbouleh

Preparation time:
  30 minutes
Cooking time:
  30 minutes
Serves 6

1 cup cracked wheat
500 g lamb mince
1/4 cup pinenuts
1 small onion, finely chopped
1 small green capsicum, finely chopped
1 teaspoon ground allspice
1/2 teaspoon ground nutmeg
1/2 teaspoon ground cinnamon
1/2 teaspoon ground chilli
1/3 cup plain yoghurt
1 egg, lightly beaten
1 cup plain yoghurt, extra
1/4 cup chopped fresh mint

Tabbouleh
1 1/2 cups chopped fresh parsley
1/2 cup chopped fresh mint
6 spring onions, chopped
4 large ripe tomatoes, peeled, seeded, chopped
1/4 cup olive oil
1 1/2 tablespoons lemon juice

1 Preheat oven to moderately hot 210°C. Brush a deep 29 x 19 x 3 cm Swiss roll tin with melted butter or oil. Place cracked wheat into a medium mixing bowl, cover with boiling water, stand 30 minutes or until soft, drain.
2 Combine cracked wheat with lamb mince, pinenuts, onion, capsicum, allspice, nutmeg, cinnamon, chilli, yoghurt and egg. Press into prepared tin. Score diamond shapes by making three straight cuts lengthways along mixture and five diagonal cuts across. Bake for 30 minutes or until well-browned, cut into diamond shapes.
3 Combine extra yoghurt and mint, serve with lamb and Tabbouleh.
4 **To make Tabbouleh:** Combine parsley, mint, spring onions and tomatoes in medium mixing bowl, add olive oil and lemon juice, stir until combined.

Note: Mince mixture can be prepared a day ahead and stored, covered in plastic wrap, in refrigerator. Cooked or uncooked mince mixture can be frozen for up to 2 months. Tabbouleh can be made up to 8 hours ahead.

Pasta with Lamb and Vegetables

Preparation time:
  15 minutes
Cooking time:
  20 minutes
Serves 4

2 tablespoons oil
1 large onion, cut into eighths
2 garlic cloves, crushed
500 g lamb mince
125 g small mushroom caps, halved
1 small red capsicum, seeded, chopped
150 g (1 cup) shelled broad beans
440 g can tomatoes
2 tablespoons tomato paste
500 g dried penne pasta
125 g feta cheese
2 tablespoons sliced fresh basil

1 Heat oil in heavy-based pan, add onion and garlic; stir-fry over medium heat for 2 minutes or until lightly browned. Add lamb mince; stir-fry over high heat for 4 minutes or until well-browned and all liquid has evaporated. Use a fork to break up any lumps as mince cooks.
2 Add mushrooms, capsicum, broad beans, undrained crushed tomatoes and tomato

Pasta with Lamb and Vegetables.

paste; bring to boil, reduce heat to a simmer, cover, cook for 10 minutes or until vegetables are tender; stir occasionally.
3 Cook pasta in large pan of rapidly boiling water, with a little oil added, until just tender, drain. Spoon into serving bowls, top with lamb and vegetable sauce, crumble cheese over sauce, sprinkle with basil.

Note: Sauce can be made up to 2 days ahead. Store, covered in plastic wrap, in refrigerator. Reheat sauce and cook pasta just before serving. Unsuitable to freeze.

37

Spicy Crêpe Stack

Preparation time:
 45 minutes
Cooking time:
 30 minutes
Serves 4

Cornmeal Crêpes
1 cup plain flour
1/2 cup fine cornmeal
1 egg, lightly beaten
1 1/2 cups water

Lamb Filling
1 tablespoon oil
1 large onion, chopped
*1 medium green
 capsicum, chopped*
2 garlic cloves, crushed
2 red chillies, chopped
350 g lamb mince
440 g can tomatoes
1/4 cup tomato paste
*310 g can red kidney
 beans, drained*

1/2 cup crème fraiche
*1/2 cup grated
 mozzarella cheese*
1/4 cup grated Parmesan

1 Preheat oven to moderate 180°C. Brush an oven tray with melted butter or oil.
To make Cornmeal Crêpes: Combine flour, cornmeal, egg and water in a blender or food processor bowl; blend for 10 seconds or until smooth.
2 Pour 3 tablespoons of mixture onto lightly greased 18 cm crêpe pan; swirl evenly over base. Cook over medium heat for 1 minute or until underside is golden. Turn crêpe over; cook other side. Transfer to a plate, cover with a tea-towel. Repeat the process with remaining batter, greasing pan when necessary. You will need to make nine crêpes for this recipe.
3 To make Lamb Filling: Heat oil in heavy-based pan, add

onion, capsicum, garlic and chilli, stir-fry over medium heat for 2 minutes or until onion is lightly browned. Add lamb mince, stir-fry over high heat for 4 minutes or until well browned and all the liquid has evaporated. Use a fork to break up any lumps as mince cooks.
Add undrained crushed tomatoes and tomato paste, bring to the boil, reduce heat to a simmer; cover, cook for 5 minutes or until the mixture has reduced and thickened; stir occasionally. Add beans and stir to mix.
4 To assemble: Place a crêpe onto prepared tray; spread with 3 teaspoons crème fraiche and one-eighth of the Lamb Filling. Repeat layering process with the remaining

Spicy Crêpe Stack.

1. *Combine flour, cornmeal, egg and water in a food processor.*

2. *Transfer each crêpe to plate, cover with tea-towel.*

crème fraiche and Lamb Filling, ending with a crêpe. Sprinkle stack with mozzarella and Parmesan cheeses; bake for 30 minutes or until heated through and golden brown.
To serve, cut crêpe stack into wedges.

Note: Crème fraiche is a thick, sharp-tasting cream, similar to sour cream but with a softer flavour.

3. For Filling, stir-fry onion, capsicum garlic and chillis; add mince and stir-fry.

4. To assemble, layer crêpes, crème fraiche and Lamb Filling.

Crispy Paprika Lamb Pie

Preparation time:
 40 minutes
Cooking time:
 45 minutes
Serves 6

Pastry
1½ cups plain flour
125 g butter
1 cup (95 g) grated
 Cheddar cheese

Filling
1 tablespoon oil
1 large onion,
 chopped
500 g lamb mince
2 teaspoons ground
 paprika
25 g dried mushroom
 soup mix
1½ cups water
2 tablespoons tomato
 sauce

Topping
3 eggs, lightly beaten
1 cup sour cream
2 tablespoons
 mayonnaise
2 tablespoons chopped
 fresh parsley

1 Preheat oven to
moderately hot 210°C.
Brush a 20 cm
springform tin with
melted butter or oil. **To
make Pastry:** Sift flour
into large mixing bowl,
add chopped butter.
Using fingertips, rub
butter into flour for
2 minutes or until
mixture is a fine and
crumbly texture. Add
cheese, stir until
combined. Reserve
1 cup of mixture for
topping. Press
remaining mixture over
base and 5 cm up side
of prepared tin.
2 To make Filling:
Heat oil in heavy-based
pan, add onion; stir-fry
over medium heat for
3 minutes or until lightly
browned. Add lamb
mince; stir-fry over high
heat for 4 minutes or
until well browned and
all the liquid has
evaporated. Use a fork to
break up any lumps as
mince cooks. Add
paprika; stir-fry
1 minute. Add soup mix,
water and tomato sauce;
stir to combine. Bring to
boil, reduce to simmer;
cook, uncovered,
5 minutes or until
mixture thickens; cool,
press into pastry shell.
3 To make Topping:
Combine eggs, sour
cream, mayonnaise and
parsley; pour over filling.
Sprinkle with reserved
pastry mixture. Bake for
45 minutes or until crisp
and golden; stand
5 minutes, remove from
tin, cut into wedges.

Tagliatelle with Lamb and Rosemary Sausage

Preparation time:
 20 minutes
Cooking time:
 20 minutes
Serves 4

500 g dried tagliatelle

Lamb and Rosemary Sausage
500 g lamb mince
1 cup (60 g) fresh white
 breadcrumbs
2 garlic cloves, crushed
1 teaspoon ground
 chillies
2 tablespoons fresh
 rosemary leaves,
 chopped
2 tablespoons oil

Sauce
2 tablespoons oil,
 extra
1 large onion, sliced
2 large (250g) ripe
 tomatoes, peeled,
 seeded, chopped
1 cup chicken stock
1 cup thickened
 cream
2 tablespoons fresh
 rosemary leaves,
 chopped
⅓ cup grated, fresh
 Parmesan cheese

1 Cook tagliatelle in
large pan of rapidly
boiling water with a little
oil added until just
tender; drain, set aside.

---

*Crispy Paprika Lamb Pie (top) and Tagliatelle with
Lamb and Rosemary Sausage.*

2 To make Lamb and Rosemary Sausage:
Combine lamb in a large mixing bowl with breadcrumbs, garlic, chilli and rosemary. Divide mixture into eight equal portions, roll each portion into a sausage shape. Heat oil in heavy-based pan, add sausages in single layer, cook over medium heat for 5 minutes or until cooked through and well-browned, turn sausages occasionally during cooking. Drain on absorbent paper, cool, cut into 1 cm slices, set aside.

3 To make Sauce:
Heat extra oil in large pan, add onion, stir-fry over medium heat for 3 minutes or until tender and lightly browned. Add tomato, stock, cream and rosemary, bring to boil, cook 1 minute. Add reserved tagliatelle and sausage slices, stir over medium heat for 2 minutes or until heated through. Serve sprinkled with cheese.

Note: Sausages can be cooked a day ahead. Tagliatelle can be cooked a day ahead, toss with a little oil to prevent strands sticking together. Store covered with plastic wrap, in refrigerator. Unsuitable to freeze.

Lamb and Apricot Roast

Preparation time:
20 minutes
Cooking time:
1 hour 15 minutes
Serves 6

2 kg leg of lamb, boned
2 tablespoons oil

Filling
200 g lamb mince
1/4 cup fresh breadcrumbs
1/4 cup chopped dried apricots
2 tablespoons fruit chutney
1 tablespoon fresh rosemary, chopped

Sauce
1 1/2 tablespoons plain flour
1 1/2 cups chicken stock
2 teaspoons seeded mustard
2 teaspoons Worcestershire Sauce
1/4 cup cream

1 Preheat oven to moderately hot 210°C. Trim excess fat from leg of lamb, lay out flat, fat side down.

2 To make Filling:
Combine lamb mince with breadcrumbs, apricots, chutney and rosemary. Press filling over lamb, fold lamb over to enclose filling. Tie at intervals with string, to retain its shape, tucking in ends.

3 Rub lamb all over with oil, place in a deep baking dish, bake for 1 hour and 15 minutes for a rare result, 1 hour 30 minutes for medium result and 1 hour 45 minutes for well-done result. Baste lamb occasionally with pan juices. Remove from oven, leave, covered with foil, in warm place for 10 minutes while preparing the sauce.

4 To make Sauce:
Scoop fat from the surface of pan juices and discard. Add flour to juices, stir until smooth, stir over medium heat 1 minute. Add combined stock, mustard and Worcestershire sauce, stir over medium heat until sauce boils and thickens, reduce heat to a simmer, cook for 3 minutes. Stir in cream.

5 Remove string from lamb, slice lamb, serve with sauce.

Note: Lamb can be filled and tied with string a day ahead. Store, covered in plastic wrap, in refrigerator.

Lamb and Apricot Roast.

Lamb Kebabs with Golden Pilaf

Preparation time:
  25 minutes
Cooking time:
  30 minutes
Makes 8

750 g lamb mince
1 small onion, finely
  chopped
2 tablespoons finely
  chopped fresh
  coriander
1 tablespoon ground
  cumin
1 teaspoon grated
  lemon rind

Golden Pilaf
3 tablespoons oil
1 teaspoon turmeric
1 medium onion,
  sliced
2 cups Basmati or
  jasmine rice
4 cups vegetable
  stock

1 Place mince, onion, coriander, cumin and lemon rind in a large mixing bowl and combine thoroughly. Divide mixture into eight equal portions and form into sausage shapes around large metal or wooden skewers. Refrigerate until required.

2 To make Golden Pilaf: Heat oil in a large pan. Add turmeric and onion and stir over medium heat for 2 minutes or until onion is soft. Add rice and continue stirring for 1 minute, until grains of rice are coated in oil.

3 Add stock; cover pan with tight-fitting lid. Bring slowly to boil; stir once. Reduce heat, simmer, covered, for 10 minutes or until almost all water is absorbed. Remove from heat, leave covered 5 minutes or until water is absorbed and rice is just tender. Stir rice with a fork to separate grains before serving.

Lamb Kebabs with Golden Pilaf.

1. Form mince into sausage shapes around metal or wooden skewers.

2. For Pilaf, stir-fry rice with onions and turmeric to coat grains of rice with oil.

4 Heat grill or frypan, brush with oil. Cook kebabs for 12 minutes, turning occasionally to brown all over. Serve on bed of Golden Pilaf.

HINT
To test seasonings when you're preparing a mince mixture, fry a teaspoonful of the mixture and taste it. Adjust salt, pepper, herbs and spices, as desired.

3. Simmer rice, covered, 10 minutes or until almost all water is absorbed.

4. Cook kebabs for 12 minutes, turning occasionally to brown all over.

Mediterranean-style Meatballs

Preparation time:
 30 minutes
Cooking time:
 35 minutes
Serves 6

750 g lamb mince
1 clove garlic, crushed
2 teaspoons dried rosemary
1/4 cup pinenuts, finely chopped
2 medium eggplant
1 tablespoon salt
2 tablespoons olive oil
2 medium onions, cut in 1 cm wedges
4 medium zucchini, cut in 1 cm slices
2 medium red capsicums, cut in 2 cm squares
2 medium green capsicums, cut in 2 cm squares
3 large tomatoes, chopped
3 tablespoons tomato paste
1 teaspoon dried oregano
1/2 cup fresh basil leaves, shredded

1 Place mince, garlic, rosemary and pinenuts in a large mixing bowl and combine thoroughly. Roll level tablespoonfuls of mixture into 36 balls. Refrigerate until required.

2 Cut eggplant into 2 cm slices, spread out in a single layer on a plate and sprinkle with salt. Set aside for 15 minutes, then rinse and dry thoroughly. Cut into 2 cm cubes. Heat oil in a large pan. Add onions and stir-fry for 3 minutes over medium heat until soft, add zucchini, eggplant and capsicums. Stir-fry for about 5 minutes, until vegetables are just tender. Add tomatoes, tomato paste and oregano, combine thoroughly. Reduce heat to low, cover, and cook for a further 15 minutes, until vegetables are very tender yet still retain their shape. Add basil.

3 Heat frypan and brush lightly with oil. Cook meatballs over medium heat for about 12 minutes, shaking pan often, until well browned. Drain on absorbent paper. Add to vegetable mixture and stir to coat meatballs in sauce. Serve with crusty bread.

Mediterranean-style Meatballs (top) and Honey and Chilli Lamb with Beans.

Honey and Chilli Lamb with Beans

Preparation time:
 15 minutes
Cooking time:
 20 minutes
Serves 4

2 tablespoons oil
500 g lamb mince
1 large onion, sliced
1 small red capsicum, cut into strips
1 small green capsicum, cut into strips
2 garlic cloves, crushed
2 red chillies, chopped
2 teaspoons grated fresh ginger
1 teaspoon ground cumin
1 teaspoon ground paprika
1 cup beef stock
1 cup tomato purée
1/3 cup honey
1/3 cup white vinegar
2 tablespoons soy sauce
440 g can lima beans, drained

1 Heat oil in heavy-based pan, add lamb mince, stir-fry over high heat for 4 minutes or until well browned and all of the liquid has evaporated. Use a fork to break up any lumps as mince cooks.

2 Add onion, red and green capsicum, garlic, chillies, ginger, cumin and paprika; stir-fry

over medium heat for
2 minutes.
3 Add stock, tomato
purée, honey, vinegar
and soy sauce; bring to
boil, reduce heat to a
simmer, cover, cook for
10 minutes. Add beans,
cook further 10 minutes
or until mixture has
reduced and thickened.

Lamb and Spinach Pie

Preparation time:
45 minutes
Cooking time:
40 minutes
Serves 6

Filling
2 tablespoons oil
1 large onion, chopped
2 garlic cloves,
  crushed
500 g lamb mince
250 g small button
  mushrooms, sliced
1 tablespoon chopped
  fresh rosemary
3/4 cup tomato purée
2 tablespoons plain flour
1 cup chicken stock
6 large spinach leaves
milk for glazing
1 tablespoon sesame
  seeds
1 tablespoon caraway
  seeds

Pastry
2 1/2 cups plain flour
185 g butter
1 egg, lightly beaten
2 tablespoons water

1 Preheat oven to
moderately hot 210°C.
Brush an oven tray with
melted butter or oil.
Heat oil in heavy-based
pan, add onion and
garlic, stir-fry over
medium heat for
2 minutes or until
lightly browned. Add
lamb mince, stir-fry
over high heat until
well-browned and all
of the liquid has
evaporated. Use a fork
to break up any lumps
as mince cooks.
2 Add mushrooms,
rosemary, tomato purée
and blended flour and
stock, stir over high
heat until boiling,
reduce heat to a simmer,
cook uncovered for
5 minutes or until most
of the liquid has
evaporated and mixture
has thickened, stir
often, cool.
3 Remove stalks from
spinach leaves; discard.
Blanch leaves in boiling
water for 3 minutes or
until tender. Rinse
under cold water; drain,
chop roughly.
4 To make Pastry:
Place flour and butter
in food processor bowl.
Using pulse action,
press button for 20
seconds or until
mixture is a fine,
crumbly texture. Add
egg and almost all the
water, process
5 seconds until mixture
is smooth, add more

water if necessary.
Leave covered with
plastic wrap, in
refrigerator for
30 minutes.
5 Turn onto lightly
floured surface, knead
1 minute or until
smooth. Roll half
pastry into a 23 cm
round, place onto
oven tray.
6 Spoon lamb filling
onto pastry leaving a
2 cm border, top with
spinach, brush border
with milk.
7 Roll remaining
pastry to a 26 cm
round, place over
filling, press edges
together, pinch frill
around edge. Brush all
over with milk, sprinkle
with sesame and
caraway seeds. Bake for
40 minutes or until
golden brown. Cut into
wedges to serve.

Nutty Lamburgers with Yoghurt Sauce

Preparation time:
20 minutes
Cooking time:
16 minutes
Serves 6

750 g lamb mince
1/2 cup walnuts, finely
  chopped
1 small onion, finely
  chopped
1 teaspoon curry powder
3 tomatoes, chopped

Lamb and Spinach Pie (top) and Nutty Lamburgers with Yoghurt Sauce.

Yoghurt Sauce
1/2 cup plain yoghurt
1/4 cup mayonnaise
1 clove garlic, crushed
1 tablespoon finely chopped mint
1 tablespoon finely chopped parsley

1 Place mince, walnuts, onion and curry powder in a large mixing bowl and combine thoroughly. Divide mixture into six equal portions and shape into patties 1½ cm thick. Cover and refrigerate until required.

2 To make Yoghurt Sauce: Combine all ingredients; refrigerate until needed.

3 Heat grill or frypan and brush lightly with oil. Cook burgers over medium-high heat for 8 minutes each side, turning once only. Serve in pita bread with chopped tomato and Yoghurt Sauce.

Chicken Mince

With people eating more chicken, and specialty chicken shops abounding, chicken mince, once only made at home in a food processor, is now readily available. Use it to make hamburgers, curries, pies and casseroles, and even sausages. Chicken mince is especially lean – perfect if you're on a low-fat diet. Remember, however, that lean meat dries out easily and should be combined with moist ingredients.

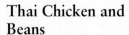

Thai Chicken and Beans

Preparation time:
  20 minutes
Cooking time:
  12 minutes
Serves 4

2 tablespoons oil
2 large red onions, cut into eighths
500 g chicken mince
1 tablespoon fish sauce
440 g can tomatoes
1 cup chicken stock
250 g beans, cut into 2.5 cm pieces
1/3 cup fresh basil, cut into strips
2 tablespoons chopped fresh coriander
1/3 cup chopped roasted peanuts

Spice Paste
2 spring onions, *chopped*
2 garlic cloves, *chopped*
2 teaspoons grated lemon rind
2 red chillies, *chopped*
3 teaspoons ground paprika
1 teaspoon ground turmeric
1 teaspoon ground cumin
1/3 cup water

1 Heat oil in heavy-based pan, add onion, stir-fry over medium heat 2 minutes or until lightly browned. Add chicken mince, stir-fry over high heat for 4 minutes or until all liquid has evaporated. Use a fork to break up lumps as mince cooks.

Thai Chicken and Beans (top) and Coconut Chicken Curry (page 52).

2 To make Spice Paste:
Combine spring onions, garlic, lemon rind, chillies, paprika, turmeric, cumin and water in food processor or blender, blend for 30 seconds or until smooth.
3 Add Spice Paste, stir-fry over high heat for 1 minute. Add fish sauce, undrained crushed tomatoes, stock and beans, bring to boil, cover, reduce heat to a simmer, cook for 5 minutes or until beans are tender. Add basil and coriander, stir until combined. Serve sprinkled with peanuts.

Coconut Chicken Curry

Preparation time:
 20 minutes
Cooking time:
 20 minutes
Serves 4

10 *Chinese dried mushrooms*
750 g *chicken mince*
2 *teaspoons finely grated ginger*
2 *tablespoons oil*
2 *large onions, cut into eighths*
400 mL *can coconut milk*
1/2 *cup water*
1 *tablespoon fish sauce*
1/4 *cup fresh basil, cut into strips*

Curry Paste
2 *fresh coriander stems with roots and leaves*
1 *stem fresh lemon grass, finely chopped*
2 *garlic cloves, chopped*
2 *teaspoons grated lemon rind*
2 *green chillies, chopped*
2 *teaspoons ground turmeric*
1/3 *cup water, extra*

1 Place mushrooms in small bowl, pour over enough boiling water to cover. Stand 20 minutes or until mushrooms are soft, drain. Discard stems, chop caps finely.
2 Combine mushrooms in medium bowl with chicken mince and ginger. Roll tablespoons of mixture into balls.
3 Heat oil in heavy-based pan, add chicken balls in single layer, cook over medium-high heat for 4 minutes or until well browned, turn often during cooking. Drain chicken balls on absorbent paper.
4 Add onion to pan, stir-fry over medium heat for 2 minutes or until lightly browned.

5 To make Curry Paste: Place coriander, lemon grass, garlic, rind, chillies, turmeric and extra water in food processor or blender, blend until smooth.
6 Add Curry Paste to onion, stir-fry for 2 minutes. Add coconut milk, water and fish sauce, stir over heat until boiling. Reduce heat to simmer, add chicken balls, cover, cook for 20 minutes or until sauce has thickened. Stir in basil.

Tandoori Chicken Burgers with Creamy Chutney

Preparation time:
 20 minutes
Cooking time:
 16 minutes
Serves 6

800 g *chicken mince*
1 *cup (60 g) fresh white breadcrumbs*
2 *teaspoons ground cumin*
2 *teaspoons ground coriander*
1 *teaspoon ground ginger*
1/2 *teaspoon garam masala*
2 *tablespoons yoghurt*
1 *tablespoon lemon juice*
1 *clove garlic*
1 *tablespoon finely chopped parsley*

Tandoori Chicken Burgers with Creamy Chutney.

Creamy Chutney
1/3 cup mango chutney
2 tablespoons yoghurt

1 Place all burger ingredients in a large mixing bowl and combine thoroughly. Divide mixture into six and shape into patties 1 cm thick. Refrigerate, covered, until required.

2 **To make Creamy Chutney:** Combine ingredients in a small bowl and refrigerate until required.
3 Heat frypan or grill and brush lightly with oil. Cook burgers over medium-high heat for 7 minutes each side, turning once only. Serve immediately with Creamy Chutney.

HINT
For instant fresh breadcrumbs, cut the crusts from slices of white bread and process in bowl of food processor or blender for about 8 seconds. Four slices of bread will give you one cup of breadcrumbs.

53

Creamy Chicken Strudel

Preparation time:
 30 minutes
Cooking time:
 30 minutes
Serves 4

1 tablespoon oil
1 large onion,
 chopped
2 garlic cloves,
 crushed
250 g chicken mince
1 tablespoon curry
 powder
⅓ cup ricotta
 cheese
¼ cup sour cream
10 sheets filo pastry
90 g butter,
 melted
1 stick of celery,
 finely chopped
1 small red capsicum,
 finely chopped
1 small avocado,
 sliced
1 tablespoon sesame
 seeds

1 Preheat oven to moderate 180°C. Brush an oven tray with melted butter or oil. Heat oil in heavy-based pan, add onion and garlic, stir-fry over medium heat for 2 minutes or until lightly browned. Add chicken mince, stir-fry over high heat for 4 minutes or until well-browned and all liquid has evaporated. Use a fork to break up any lumps of mince as it cooks. Add curry powder, stir-fry for 1 minute, cool. Combine chicken mixture with ricotta cheese and sour cream.

2 Place a sheet of pastry on work surface, brush all over with melted butter. Place another sheet of pastry on top, brush all over with butter. Repeat with remaining pastry and butter.
3 Spoon chicken mixture along the long side of the pastry. Top with celery, capsicum and avocado.
4 Roll up, tucking in ends. Place, seam-side down, on prepared tray, brush with butter, sprinkle with sesame seeds. Bake for 30 minutes or until pastry is golden brown. Serve sliced.

Creamy Chicken Strudel.

HINT
The chicken mixture can be prepared a day ahead and stored, covered in plastic wrap, in refrigerator. Assemble the strudel just before cooking, keeping the pastry covered with a damp cloth to prevent sheets drying out. It is unsuitable to freeze.

1. Add curry powder to chicken mixture, stir-fry 1 minute, cool.

2. Place one sheet of pastry on work surface, brush all over with butter.

. Top chicken mixture with celery,
apsicum and avocado.

4. Place strudel, seam-side down, on
prepared tray.

Chicken and Corn Sausages with Salsa Cruda

Preparation time:
 20 minutes
Cooking time:
 35 minutes
Makes 12

800g chicken mince
1 cup (60 g) fresh
 breadcrumbs
130g can creamed corn
1 tablespoon fresh
 chives, finely chopped
1/4 cup cornmeal

Salsa Cruda
2 large tomatoes, finely
 chopped
1 medium onion, finely
 chopped
1 clove garlic,
 crushed
2 tablespoons fresh
 coriander, finely
 chopped
1 tablespoon orange
 juice

1 Preheat oven to
moderate 180°C. Line
an oven tray with
aluminium foil and
brush lightly with oil.
Place mince,
breadcrumbs, corn,
chives and cornmeal in
a large mixing bowl and
combine thoroughly.
Divide into 12 equal
portions and shape into
sausages about 13 cm
long. Mixture will be
quite moist.

2 To make Salsa:
Combine all ingredients
in a small bowl and
refrigerate for at least
1 hour for flavours to
combine. Serve at room
temperature.
3 Place sausages on
prepared tray and bake
for 35 minutes, turning
occasionally during
cooking. Serve with
Salsa Cruda.

Chicken Tortillas

Preparation time:
 30 minutes
Cooking time:
 25 minutes
Serves 4

Tortillas
1 cup finely ground
 cornmeal
1 cup plain flour
60 g butter
1/2 cup water

Topping
1 tablespoon oil
125 g chicken mince
125 g chorizo sausage,
 chopped
2 teaspoons sambal
 oelek (chilli paste)
1 large onion, chopped
1 medium green
 capsicum, seeded and
 chopped
1/3 cup tomato paste
1 cup grated Cheddar
 cheese

1 Preheat oven to
moderate 180°C. Brush
two oven trays with
melted butter or oil. To
make Tortillas: Place
cornmeal, flour and
butter in food processor.
Using pulse action, press
button for 20 seconds
or until mixture is fine
and crumbly. Add
almost all the water,
process 5 seconds or
until mixture is
combined. Add enough
water to give a soft
dough. Turn onto
lightly-floured surface,
knead for 1 minute or
until smooth.
2 Divide dough into
eight portions, roll each
out to a 10 cm circle.
Place onto oven trays,
bake for 15 minutes.
3 To make Topping:
Heat oil in heavy-based
pan, add chicken mince
and sausage, stir-fry
over high heat for
4 minutes or until
well-browned and all
liquid has evaporated.
Use a fork to break up
any lumps as mince
cooks. Add sambal
oelek, onion and
capsicum, stir-fry for
3 minutes or until tender
4 Spread tortillas with
tomato paste, top with
chicken mixture,
sprinkle with cheese.
Bake for 10 minutes or
until lightly browned.

*Chicken and Corn Sausages with Salsa Cruda (to
and Chicken Tortilla*

Chicken Hot Pot

Preparation time:
20 minutes
Cooking time:
20 minutes
Serves 4

500 g chicken mince
50 g sachet dried cream
of chicken soup
2 tablespoons oil
2 large onions, sliced
2 large potatoes, cut
into 2 cm cubes
4 medium carrots, cut
into 1 cm slices
1 cup white wine
3 cups water
1¼ cups thickened
cream

1 Combine chicken
mince and soup mix in
small mixing bowl, roll
tablespoons of mixture
into balls.
2 Heat oil in
heavy-based pan, add
chicken balls in single
layer, cook on all sides
over medium heat for
5 minutes or until
well browned. Remove
from pan, drain on
absorbent paper.
3 Add onion, potato
and carrot to pan,
stir-fry over medium
heat 4 minutes or until
lightly browned. Add
wine, water and cream.
Return chicken balls to

pan, bring to the boil,
reduce heat to a simmer,
cook uncovered for
20 minutes or until
vegetables are tender
and sauce has reduced
and thickened, stirring
occasionally.

Note: This dish can be
cooked two days ahead,
and can be frozen for
two months.

Chicken and Sweet Potato Pie

Preparation time:
30 minutes
Cooking time:
20 minutes
Serves 6

1 tablespoon oil
1 large onion, chopped
750 g chicken mince
750 g (about
3 medium) kumara
(sweet potato),
chopped
250 g button
mushrooms, halved
1½ cups chicken stock
440 g can tomatoes
½ cup tomato purée
2 tablespoons fresh
thyme leaves
1 tablespoon
Worcestershire Sauce

Topping
4 large (1.2 kg) old
potatoes, chopped
60 g butter
½ cup sour cream

1 Preheat oven to
moderate 180°C. Heat
oil in heavy-based pan,
add onion, stir-fry over
medium heat for
2 minutes or until
lightly browned. Add
mince, stir-fry over high
heat for 4 minutes or
until well browned
and all liquid has
evaporated. Use a fork
to break up any lumps
as mince cooks.
2 Add kumara,
mushrooms, stock,
undrained crushed
tomatoes, tomato
purée, thyme and
Worcestershire Sauce.
Bring to boil, reduce
heat to simmer, cover,
cook 15 minutes or
until mixture has
thickened and kumara
is tender. Spoon into
24 cm pie plate.
3 To make Topping:
Cook potatoes in
rapidly boiling water
for 10 minutes or until
tender, drain. Place in
large bowl with butter
and sour cream, mash
with a fork or vegetable
masher until smooth
and fluffy. Spread
topping over chicken
filling, using a fork.
Bake for 20 minutes or
until heated through
and lightly browned.

*Chicken Hot Pot (top) and Chicken and Sweet
Potato Pie.*

Pasta Shells with Chicken and Pesto

Preparation time:
  30 minutes
Cooking time:
  15 minutes
Serves 4

*20 dried giant pasta
  shells (about
  5 cm long)
2 tablespoons oil
2 leeks, sliced
500 g chicken mince
1 tablespoon plain
  flour
1 cup chicken stock
1/3 cup chopped
  pimiento
1/2 cup (40 g) grated
  fresh Parmesan
  cheese*

Pesto
*1 cup fresh
  basil
1/4 cup pinenuts
2 cloves garlic,
  crushed
1/4 cup olive oil*

1 Preheat oven to moderate 180°C. Brush a shallow baking dish with melted butter or oil. Cook pasta shells in a large pan of rapidly boiling water, with a little oil added to prevent sticking, until they are just tender; drain.
2 Heat oil in heavy-based pan, add leeks, stir-fry over medium heat for 2 minutes or until they are soft. Add the chicken mince, cook over high heat for 4 minutes until well-browned and all liquid has evaporated. Use a fork to break up any lumps as mince cooks. Add flour, stir over heat 1 minute. Add stock and pimiento, stir over medium heat until boiling, reduce heat to a simmer, cook 1 minute or until mixture has reduced and thickened.
3 To make Pesto: Place basil, pinenuts, garlic and oil in food processor bowl or blender. Blend for 30 seconds or until smooth. Spoon into a small bowl or jug, press plastic wrap over surface of pesto to exclude any air.
4 To assemble: Spoon the chicken mixture into cooked pasta shells, place into prepared baking dish, cover with aluminium foil. Bake 15 minutes or until heated through. Serve topped with a spoonful of pesto; sprinkle with cheese.

Pasta Shells with Chicken and Pesto

1. Cook pasta shells in pan of rapidly boiling water.

2. Stir-fry leek over medium heat for 2 minutes.

3. For Pesto, blend basil, pinenuts, garlic and oil until smooth.

4. Spoon chicken mixture into pasta shells, bake 15 minutes.

Chicken and Waldorf Salad Rolls

Preparation time:
20 minutes
Cooking time:
5 minutes
Serves 4

1 tablespoon oil
125 g chicken
 mince
2 spring onions,
 chopped
1 small green apple,
 chopped
1 stick of celery,
 chopped
2 tablespoons chopped
 walnuts
¼ cup mayonnaise
2 tablespoons sour
 cream
4 bread rolls
1 large ripe tomatoes,
 sliced
4 lettuce leaves

1 Heat oil in heavy-based pan, add chicken mince, stir-fry over high heat for 4 minutes or until well-browned and all liquid has evaporated. Use a fork to break up any lumps of mince as it cooks. Add spring onions, stir-fry 1 minute, cool.
2 Combine chicken mixture with apple, celery, walnuts, mayonnaise and sour cream.

3 Slice tops off bread rolls, scoop out most of the bread.
4 Spoon chicken mixture into bread rolls to half-fill them. Top with tomato slices and lettuce leaves, spoon over remaining chicken mixture, replace tops of rolls.

Note: Take advantage of juices and flavours remaining from cooking rissoles by re-using frypan to make sauce.

Chicken Rissoles with Creamy Mushroom Sauce

Preparation time:
25 minutes
Cooking time:
26 minutes
Serves 6

1 kg chicken mince
1 cup (60 g) fresh
 breadcrumbs
1 tablespoon dried
 tarragon
1 small onion, finely
 chopped
¼ cup mayonnaise

*Creamy Mushroom
Sauce*
40 g butter
3 spring onions,
 finely chopped
300 g button
 mushrooms, sliced
¼ cup white wine
¾ cup cream

1 Place chicken mince, breadcrumbs, tarragon, onion and mayonnaise into a large mixing bowl and combine thoroughly. Divide mixture into six equal portions and shape into 1½ cm-thick patties.
2 Heat a large frypan and brush lightly with oil. Cook rissoles over medium-high heat for 8 minutes each side, turning once only. Cook in batches if necessary; do not overcrowd pan. Remove from frypan and keep warm while preparing sauce.
3 **To make Sauce:** Melt butter in frypan. Add spring onions and mushrooms and stir-fry over medium heat for 5 minutes or until soft. Add wine and cream; reduce heat to low and simmer uncovered for 10-12 minutes until sauce has reduced and thickened slightly. Serve immediately.

Chicken and Waldorf Salad Rolls (top) and Chicken Rissoles with Creamy Mushroom Sauce.

Index

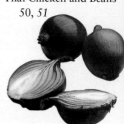